Weather in Fall

Katie Peters

GRL Consultant Diane Craig,
Certified Literacy Specialist

Lerner Publications ◆ Minneapolis

Note from a GRL Consultant
This Pull Ahead leveled book has been carefully designed for beginning readers. A team of guided reading literacy experts has reviewed and leveled the book to ensure readers pull ahead and experience success.

Lerner Publications
An imprint of Lerner Publishing Group, Inc.
241 First Avenue North
Minneapolis, MN 55401 USA

For reading levels and more information, look up this title at www.lernerbooks.com.

Main body text set in Memphis Pro 24/39
Typeface provided by Linotype.

Photo Acknowledgments
The images in this book are used with the permission of: © Elenathewise/iStockphoto, p. 3; © skynesher/iStockphoto, pp. 4–5; © PH888/Shutterstock Images, pp. 6–7; © AVTG/iStockphoto, pp. 8–9, 16 (clouds); © sueuy song/iStockphoto, pp. 10–11, 16 (wind); © Evgeny Atamanenko/Shutterstock Images, pp. 12–13, 16 (rain); © Gins Wang/ iStockphoto, pp. 14–15.

Front Cover: © FatCamera/iStockphoto

Library of Congress Cataloging-in-Publication Data

Names: Peters, Katie, author.
Title: Weather in fall / by Katie Peters.
Description: Minneapolis : Lerner Publications, [2024] | Series: Let's look at fall (pull ahead readers - nonfiction) | Includes index. | Audience: Ages 4–7 | Audience: Grades K–1 | Summary: "The air turns cool in the fall. Decodable nonfiction text and appealing photographs teach young readers about fall weather. Pairs with the fiction text Feels like Fall"—Provided by publisher.
Identifiers: LCCN 2022033565 (print) | LCCN 2022033566 (ebook) | ISBN 9781728491288 (library binding) | ISBN 9798765603185 (paperback) | ISBN 9781728498140 (ebook)
Subjects: LCSH: Autumn—Juvenile literature. | Weather—Juvenile literature.
Classification: LCC QB637.7 .P427 2024 (print) | LCC QB637.7 (ebook) | DDC 508.2—dc23/ eng20221020

LC record available at https://lccn.loc.gov/2022033565
LC ebook record available at https://lccn.loc.gov/2022033566

Manufactured in the United States of America
1 – CG – 7/15/23

Table of Contents

Weather in Fall

The weather changes
in the fall.

It gets colder in the fall.

It is cloudy in the fall.

It is windy in the fall.

It is rainy in the fall.

I like fall weather!

What does fall weather feel like where you live?

Did You See It?

clouds

rain

wind

Index

After Reading

Ask students questions about the book and the book's topic:
1. How does the weather change where you live?
2. What season do you like best?
3. What was your favorite part of the book?

Word Study

High-Frequency Word Practice
Teacher directions: Give each student a dry-erase board and marker. Have students practice writing the words "in," "it," and "the." Have students say each word as they write it.

Blending
Teacher directions: Use the following words to model how to blend words. Say each sound segment in a word and ask students to say the blended word.

fall: /f/ /a/ /ll/
get: /g/ /e/ /t/
like: /l/ /i/ /ke/

Example: fall
Teacher says: /f/ /a/ /ll/
What word do you hear?

Let's Look at Fall

What do you do in the fall? Do you start a new year of school? Do you pick apples or pumpkins? Do you watch what happens in nature? Explore fall with these fun books!

Don't miss these other Let's Look at Fall books!

PAIR IT

Nonfiction + Fiction

At the Apple Orchard + Picking Apples

At the Pumpkin Patch + Tractor Ride

Ready for School + Let's Go to School

Trees in Fall + Raking Leaves

Weather in Fall + Feels Like Fall

What Animals Do in Fall + Beaver Bev

ISBN 979-8-7656-0318-5

90000

9 798765 603185

www.lernerbooks.com

GRL: B